It's OK, Grandpop

How Brain Disease Can Open Your Mind to Acceptance

Written by
Janice Zuppa Benacchio

Halo
PUBLISHING
INTERNATIONAL

Illustrated by
Kaitlyn Benacchio

Halo Publishing International
7550 WIH-10 #800, PMB 2069,
San Antonio, TX 78229

First Edition, August 2024
ISBN: 978-1-63765-651-8
Library of Congress Control Number: 2024914224

Halo Publishing International is a self-publishing company that publishes adult fiction and
non-fiction, children's literature, self-help, spiritual, and faith-based books. Do you have a
book idea you would like us to consider publishing? Please visit www.halopublishing.com for
more information.

To donate or learn more about PSP or other neurological diseases, visit:
Cure PSP: https://www.psp.org/
American Brain Foundation: https://www.americanbrainfoundation.org/
Parkinson's Foundation: https://www.parkinson.org/
Alzheimer's Association: https://www.alz.org/alzheimers-dementia/what-is-alzheimers
MSA Coalition: https://www.multiplesystematrophy.org/about-msa/

Testimonials

The hummingbird is a symbol of PSP

"As a neurologist, I find it a great challenge to educate families about Progressive Supranuclear Palsy (PSP). It is even more difficult to explain the disease to children. In this book, Janice Zuppa Benacchio (author) and Kaitlyn Benacchio (illustrator) created an invaluable resource for parents, educators, and healthcare professionals seeking to teach children about PSP and degenerative brain disease in general. *It's OK, Grandpop* is an informative and compassionate book describing the struggles of coping with brain diseases. I highly recommend the book for families whose loved ones have PSP or similar diseases."

-Neurologist Prof. Roy Alcalay, Columbia University Medical Center (and Grandpop physician)

"As a neurologist, I highly recommend this children's book for its unique perspective narrated through the eyes of a child grappling with a family member's illness. Through its heartfelt storytelling and vivid illustrations, the book gently guides young readers through the emotional journey of dealing with progressive diseases in a loved one. By offering insight and understanding, it empowers children to navigate these difficult situations with resilience, compassion, and love. This book is a remarkable resource for families, educators, and healthcare professionals seeking to support children through challenging times."

-Dr. Sandie Worley, Movement Disorders Neurologist, Columbia University Medical Center

To my favorite person,
my guardian angel–Grandpop.

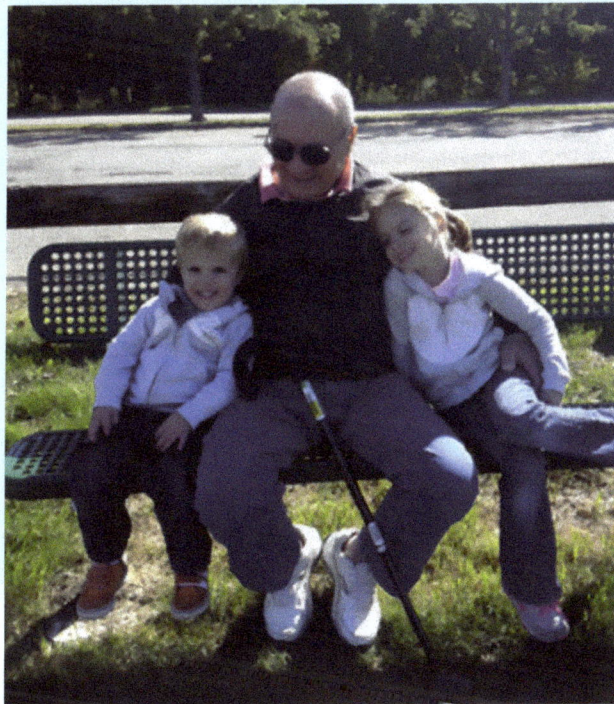

My brother, Kevin; my grandpop,
Michael J. Zuppa; and me at the park in 2015.

This is my grandpop. I loved spending time with him. He was my biggest fan, and I thought the world of him. We did everything together. We chased each other around the backyard, built the tallest LEGO towers, sang songs, and took long walks in the neighborhood.

My mother says that when I was a little girl, I preferred him over anyone else!

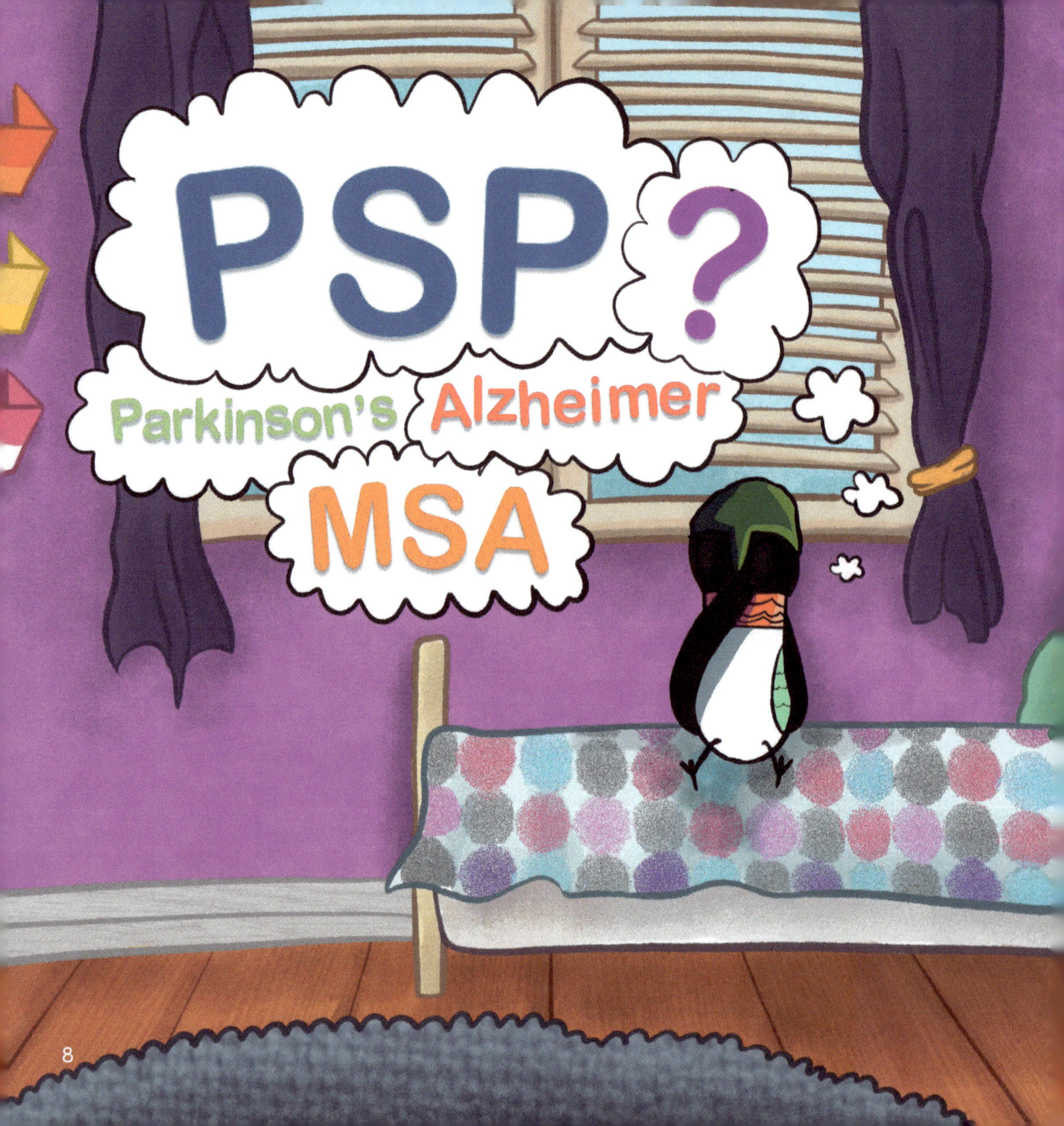
PSP?
Parkinson's
Alzheimer
MSA

When I was six years old, my grandpop was diagnosed with a rare brain disease called progressive supranuclear palsy (PSP).

I wasn't exactly sure what that meant, but over the years, I noticed my grandpop began to change.

My grandpop and I loved to visit the playground. He pushed me high on the swings and caught me on my way down the slide.

But then he began losing his balance, and he couldn't always be next to me.

"It's OK, Grandpop. You can watch me from the bench and keep your eye on me."

My grandpop loved to hold my hand and take me for long walks around the neighborhood. We had fun exploring nature and picking up sticks and rocks along the way.

But over time, his legs became weak, and he needed a walker to move around.

"It's OK, Grandpop. I will stay close to you and always be at your side."

My grandpop and I enjoyed playing board games together. I'm pretty sure he always let me win.

But, one day, his fingers stopped working, and he couldn't hold the pieces in his hands anymore.

"It's OK, Grandpop. I will always make time for you and help you along the way."

My grandpop and I loved to eat sweets. Cookies, brownies, and carrot cake with cream cheese frosting were our favorites.

But eventually he couldn't swallow foods, and his meals had to be puréed.

"It's OK, Grandpop. I know you miss sharing our special treats, but we can still share time with each other."

I loved when my grandpop carried me. I stretched out my arms, and he held me close.

But soon his legs stopped working, and he needed to stay in a wheelchair.

"It's OK, Grandpop. I can push you around and maybe even get a ride on your lap."

My grandpop loved to look at me. He bragged to his friends about how beautiful I was.

But in time, his eyes couldn't move around, and he lost the ability to focus.

"It's OK, Grandpop. I know you can still hear my voice, and you look forward to our visits."

My grandpop had the best smile and always wore one when I was around.

But, one day, his muscles grew weaker, and his smile disappeared.

"It's OK, Grandpop. I can still see your face light up when I enter the room."

My grandpop used to ask me questions about my day. We had the best conversations!

But eventually he no longer had a voice.

"It's OK, Grandpop. I will keep talking to you because I know you want to hear how I am doing."

My grandpop spent his last few days lying in bed. Although he was very still, he knew I was there with him. I told my grandpop that I love him and will miss him.

"It's OK, Grandpop. I know you will always be with me, and you are watching over me."

www.ingramcontent.com/pod-product-compliance
Lightning Source LLC
Chambersburg PA
CBHW040851100426
42813CB00015B/2776